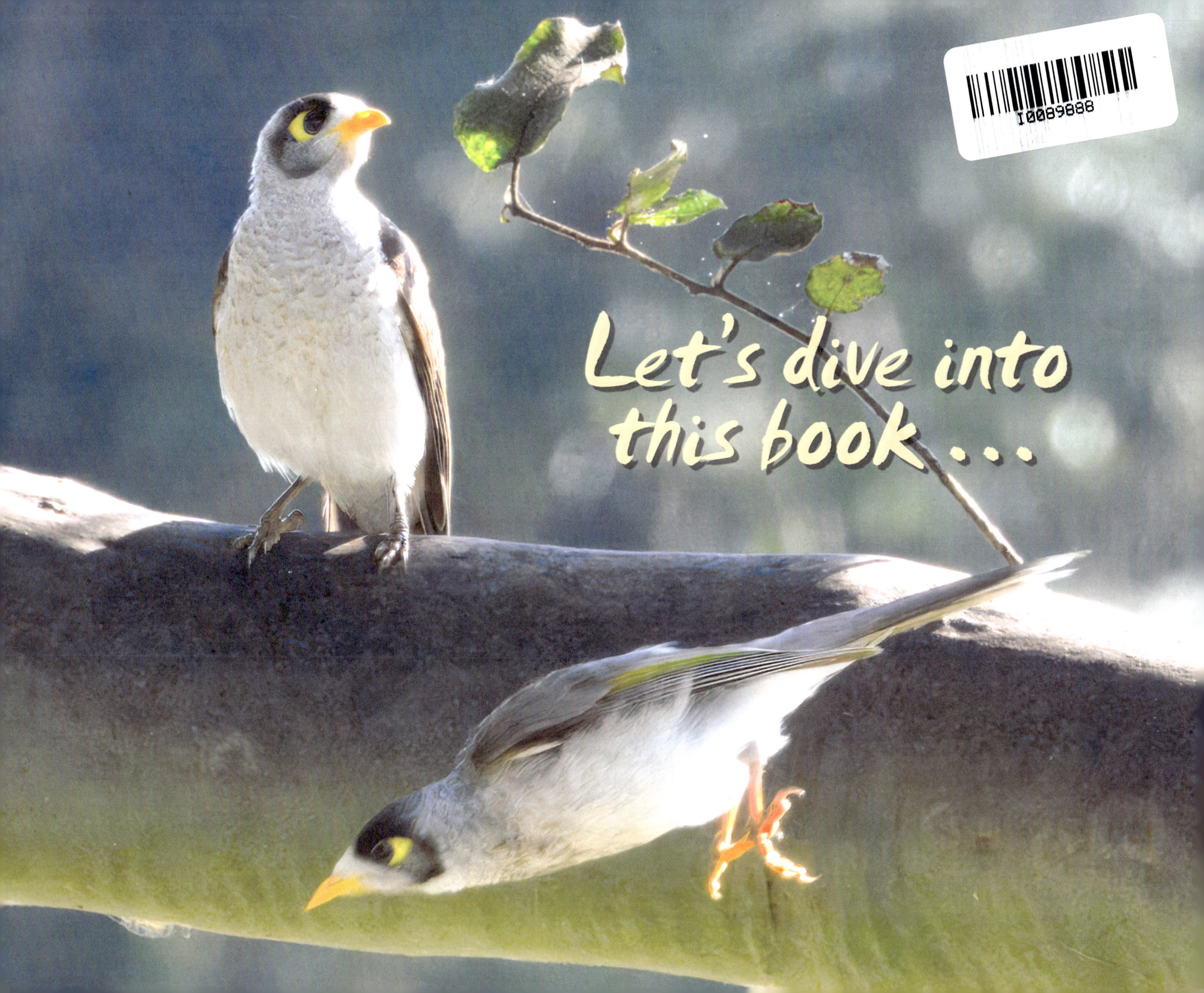
Let's dive into
this book ...

First Published 2025 by Jenny Dyer
For further information
contact through facebook pages

Walking with Wildlife
and
JD's Snaps and Designs

Text: © Jennifer Dyer 2024
Photography: © Jennifer Dyer 2024

ISBN 978-1-7637939-4-1

Cover and Artwork: Jenny Dyer

Walking with Wildlife ™

Written by Jenny Dyer

Photography and design by Jenny Dyer

I was up bright and early this morning just around sunrise and went out to check what wildlife was around.

The crested pigeons are also early risers and I found them on the old horse yard rails preening and smooching.

I have lived in this little valley for a long, long time and I can tell you … no two days are exactly the same.

Actually I grew up in this same road and now I'm a grandma and I'm still here teaching my grandson about nature and how to observe and photograph it.

Enough about me … would you care to join me again on a walk with wildlife? Walking slowly, I like to stop and spy all the little insects and lizards too but I love the birds, especially these two crested pigeons, with their pretty coloured wings which glow in the sunlight.

Wow! Have you ever seen such beautiful orange eyes and shiny, iridescent feathers? What other colours can you see in the feathers?

Another NEW bird! It makes my day to find this newby which must be a migratory species.

Well, there's an interesting story to this spangled drongo. I started photographing him and he wasn't paying much attention to me. I could hear something rustling in the bark. I looked and it was only a grey-crowned babbler (a dime a dozen ... I see them all the time) and the spangled drongo was in such beautiful light so I continued to photograph him as he shifted a few times ...

Then the spangled drongo slid from view, so I focused on the babbler who had found his breakfast in the bark. But before I could click, the drongo came swooping down so swiftly, chased the babbler and stole that fat, juicy spider from the grey-crowned babbler.

He returned to a branch in the shade to devour the spider. What a delicious, easy meal for the spangled drongo!

Do you feel sorry for that hard-working babbler?

Grey-crowned babblers are skilful hunters of insects, grubs and spiders, especially around your home. He pecked this spider out of the wood of the hollow log.

What insects have you seen being eaten by a bird?

Why do you think birds eat their insects quickly?

Do you think this grey-crowned babbler will share his food with his mate?

Well, that was a nice bath! I'd better go check if I need deodorant.

Do you ever try to imagine what the birds are saying? It can be funny to make up a conversation or story.

What do YOU think they were saying?

Noisy miners are also very good at catching insects.

Before eating them they shake them so hard that their insides come outside. Have you seen a bird do that before?

Unfortunately for the noisy miner he dropped his insect and another bird swooped down and stole his feed.

How do you think he feels?

Do you think birds feel?

Noisy miners are renowned for chasing other birds away. Here is one with a pied currawong. Look at him trying to psych out the bigger bird.

Now he's harassing a
magpie. It's a bit
ambitious though.

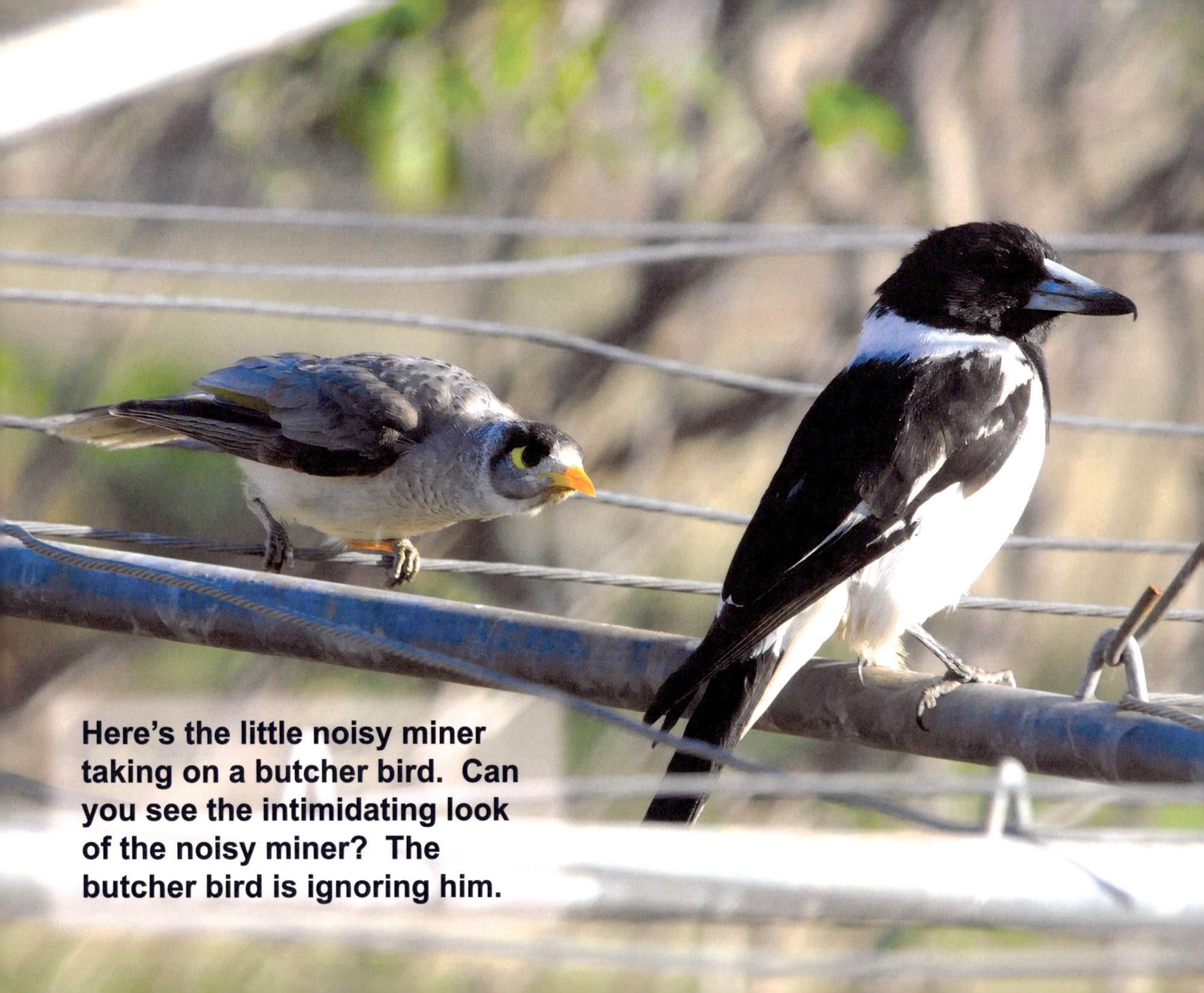

Here's the little noisy miner taking on a butcher bird. Can you see the intimidating look of the noisy miner? The butcher bird is ignoring him.

Next, this bully comes in to chase a babbler away. Believe it or not but the grey-crowned babbler brought in reinforcements and they chased the noisy miners away but it's always a battle over their territory for these rivals.

This time the noisy miner comes in and manages to chase the grey-crowned babbler away. The battle over whose home it is continues.

Surprise!

We found
this beetle
pushed onto the
barbed wire fence.
Kookaburras or
butcher birds will save
their feed like this for later.
They also stab them on
sticks.

This mother kookaburra is ready to feed a skink to her young one. Skinks drop their tails off when they feel threatened, hoping their attacker will go after the dropped tail instead of them.

You can often hear kookaburras laughing … so his full name is "Laughing Kookaburra". They call to say "This is my territory … stay away!"

They live in the forest country near my home and will come out to hunt for food.

They can live for up to twenty years and the male and female will mate for life.

You will often see them perched upon a branch, power line or post, looking for something scrumptious to eat. Will it be a bug, beetle, lizard, snake, frog, small mammal, rodent or worm for lunch today? What a diet!

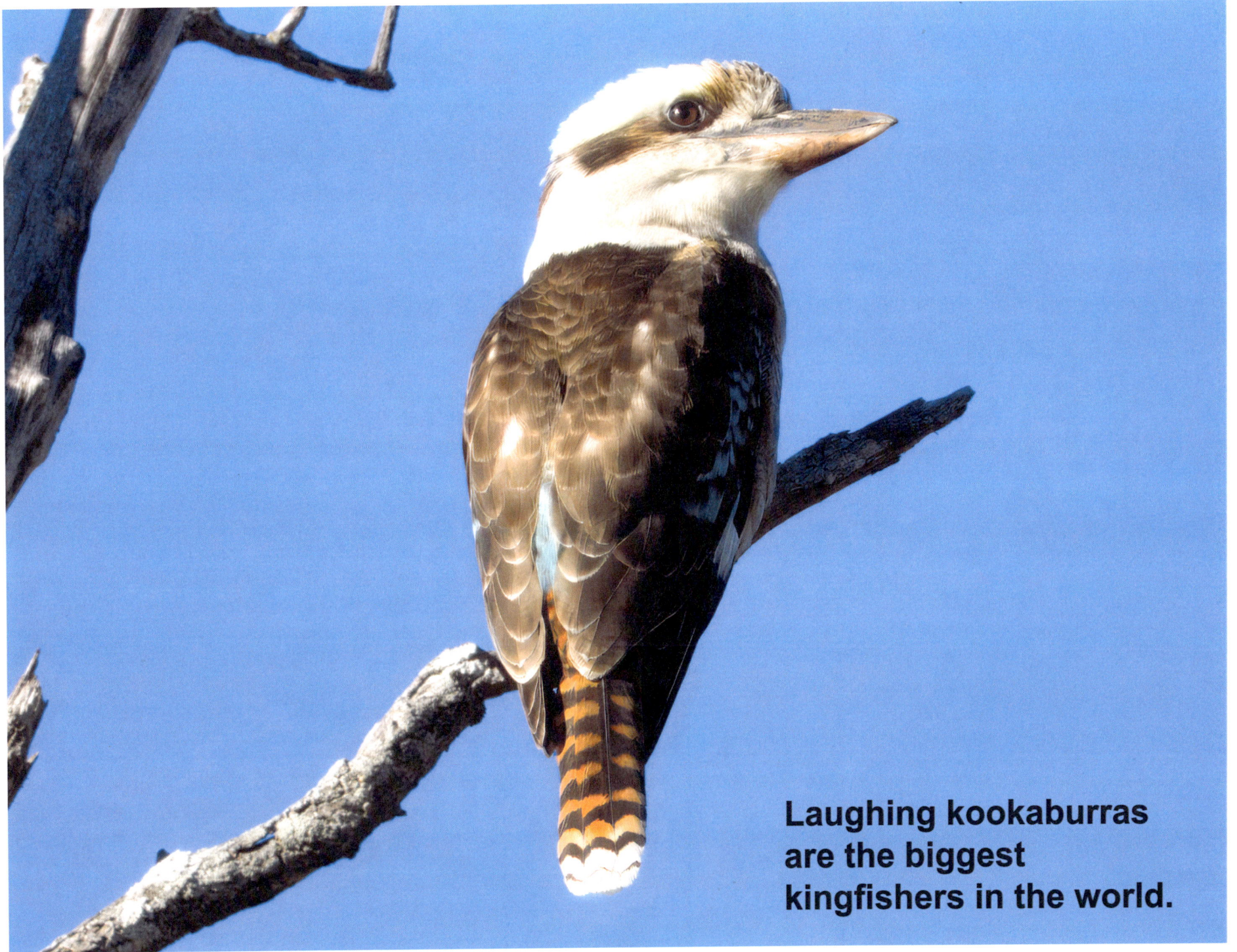

Laughing kookaburras
are the biggest
kingfishers in the world.

We came up the flat and could just see a dingo down in the gully looking up at us. Dingoes can be aggressive so we decided not to get too close. She was a healthy, young dingo and took off quickly down the gully. There have been two dingoes hanging around lately and you can hear them howling up in the hills in the early morning (dingoes don't bark).

We found a Black-faced Cuckooshrike in the big gully with a grasshopper he had just caught in his mouth. They eat mainly insects and other invertebrates. (Invertebrates have no backbone and are cold-blooded.)

Have you ever wondered where birds go when it's raining? This poor black-faced cuckooshrike just sat in the rain.

Some birds shelter in trees, nests and are even known to come in on your veranda.

My grandson was quick to spot these dragonflies and we both stopped to photograph them. I wonder if these dragonflies will become a meal for a bird like the black-faced cuckooshrike. This one is called a Graphic Flutterer.

This dragonfly is a mature male Blue Skimmer.

Further down the road on a grassy flat, we spotted a family of double-barred finches feeding on grass seed. They like the hard seeds.

Can you work out what is happening in this photo?

No, I didn't turn the photo up-side down however there is a photo hint in a few pages, but if you still can't work it out … see page 46 for the answer.

They feed on grass seed of different types, sometimes on the ground.

These birds find drinking water in an old trough, the gully or even in a pothole in the middle of the road.

White-faced herons often come in to drink at the old cattle trough as well.

I also see them walking through the paddock picking up insects.

This heron likes to hang out near the dam where he hopes to catch some fish.

I first saw the bee-eaters in a tree on the flat in the morning.

Later that afternoon I went outside and here they were sitting on our power line. Rainbow bee-eaters can eat up to 300 insects in a day.

When they spot an insect, they dive quickly and acrobatically from the power line to catch their next feed.

Bees store pollen on their legs which they transport from flower to flower and also back to their hives for food.

Bees have a second stomach called a "honey stomach" in which they carry the honey back to the hive.

Bees actually have a proboscis (tongue) to suck and lap up the nectar, and yes, it's red!

A swarm of European bees on an old fence post looking for a new hive. Maybe I was a little too close to this swarm as their sting can be dangerous.

European Bees often locate their hives in hollow branches in trees.

Can you name these birds, animals and insects?

Grey-crowned babbler

Black-faced cuckooshrike

Crested pigeon

Dingo

Laughing Kookaburra

Dragonfly

European Bee

Rainbow bee-eater

White-faced Heron

Pied Currawong

Noisy Miner

Spangled Drongo

Answer to Page 41

It's the reflection of the double-barred finch in a cattle trough. A rail covered the double-barred finch so you couldn't see him.

I am interested to hear your stories too. To participate in some upcoming competitions about wildlife, please join my Facebook page …

Walking with Wildlife

www.ingramcontent.com/pod-product-compliance
Lightning Source LLC
Chambersburg PA
CBRC091226020426
42333CB00010B/81